PUFFIN BOOKS

THE PUFFIN BOOK OF WORLD MYTHS AND LEGENDS

Anita Nair is the author of the bestselling novels *The Better Man* and *Ladies Coupé*. Her books for children include *Who Let Nonu Out?*, *Living Next Door to Alise* and *The Puffin Book of Magical Indian Myths*.

THE PUFFIN BOOK OF

World Myths and Legends

ANITA NAIR

Illustrations by Sujasha Dasgupta

PUFFIN BOOKS

PUFFIN BOOKS

USA | Canada | UK | Ireland | Australia
New Zealand | India | South Africa | China

Puffin Books is part of the Penguin Random House group of companies
whose addresses can be found at global.penguinrandomhouse.com

Published by Penguin Random House India Pvt. Ltd
7th Floor, Infinity Tower C, DLF Cyber City,
Gurgaon 122 002, Haryana, India

First published in Puffin by Penguin Random House India 2004

10 9 8 7 6 5 4 3 2 1

ISBN 9780143334774

This edition is for sale throughout the World except in Europe

Typeset in Goudy Old Style by Mantra Virtual Services, New Delhi
Printed at Replika Press Pvt. Ltd, India

www.penguinbooksindia.com

For Maitreya

Joy to the world and me

And for Dhanush, Siddarth and Sugar

Contents

ACKNOWLEDGEMENTS

As reference pointers I have drawn from:

A Classical Dictionary of Hindu Mythology and Religion by John Dowson, Rupa & Co., India;

A Dictionary of World Mythology by Arthur Cotterell, Book Club Associates, London;

Swedish Folk Tales and Legends edited by Lone Thygesen Blecher and George Blecher, Pantheon Books, New York;

The Serpent Prince: Folktales from Northeastern Thailand told by Kermit Krueger, The World Publishing Company, New York and Cleveland;

Myths of the Hindus and Buddhists by Ananda K. Coomaraswamy and Sister Nivedita, George G. Harrap & Company.

Dear Child,

Just as the myths and legends in this book are slowly losing their place in our lives, many animals too will soon disappear from our forests. With this book, it is my endeavour to do my little bit for keeping alive both the animals and the myths. I hope you will enjoy reading this collection of myths from around the world ... and I'm sure you will treasure the thought that by buying this book you have helped in preserving some of the endangered species of Indian wildlife. [A certain amount of the sum you pay to acquire this book will go to the Wildlife Trust of India.]

I'm glad you have joined hands with me in this project.

Happy Reading.

Bangalore
January 2004

Anita Nair

WHY PEOPLE BEGAN TO LIVE IN HOUSES

A Zambian Legend

Once upon a time, the great god Leza called the honey bird and gave it three calabashes, all of them closed at both ends. He told the honey bird, 'Here are three calabashes. Take them to the human beings on the earth. Two of them contain seeds. But this third one is not to be opened. Tell them, they mustn't open it until I tell them to.'

The honey bird flew all the way from heaven to the earth. On its way it kept thinking of the third calabash and with every passing moment, the bird became more and more curious. So, finally, the honey bird opened the calabashes. The first two contained seeds, as Leza had said, but the third one held death, sickness, all kinds of dangerous animals, snakes and reptiles. The honey bird didn't know what to do. Leza saw the calabash had been opened and hurried to earth.But no matter how hard they tried, they couldn't capture any of the animals or reptiles.

Suddenly the earth was a different place. During the day men and women had to tread carefully, for dangerous animals prowled everywhere. At night they were scared to sleep on the ground, for snakes and other reptiles crawled into their beds and bit them. The people realized that there was no escaping death or illness but at least they could defend themselves from the predators who sought them as food. From then on, to protect themselves, men and women began to build shelters and live in homes.

THE STORY OF NANNA, THE MOON

A Mesopotamian Legend

Enlil, the god of air, was a great lover of beauty. Even when he was a child, his eyes always sought beauty and when he saw it, he couldn't go past without caressing it. He made the tops of trees ruffle and flowers dance. He gathered waves in his mouth and blew them out as spray. He made fish shimmer and butterflies dance. When Enlil came their way, all living creatures felt a great surge of happiness. For where Enlil was, there was beauty.

When he became a young man, Enlil decided to build the most beautiful city in the world. But first he needed to find a place that would be perfect for such a city. So he travelled far and wide, seeking such a place. Then, one day, as he blew over the middle world between heaven, where the gods lived, and the dark realms of the nether world, he saw a sight that made him pause. Between the rivers Tigris and Euphrates was the most beautiful place he had ever seen. The water from the rivers fed the land, making it rich and fertile. All kinds of wonderful flowers and delicious fruits grew here. The birds sang all day and the bees, drunk with nectar, buzzed around lazily. Enlil stood there for a long time, gazing at the beauty of the place, and decided to build his city here.

When Enlil had finished building the most beautiful city in the world, he named it Nippur. Next, he decided it was time to find the most beautiful woman in the world and make her his wife. Once again, he set out on a search and in the course of his travels, met a young goddess called Ninlil. She was the prettiest woman he had seen and he fell deeply in love with her. He followed her to her house and waited at her door all day. Soon Ninlil found she couldn't stay inside her house any longer. The presence of the air god outside made it terribly windy. Windows wouldn't stay closed, the doors slammed and everything inside the house kept flying this way and that. Chairs, tables, pots and pans and even her pet cat whirled around the house. So Ninlil rushed outside and begged the air god to leave. 'But how can I go?' Enlil asked.

Ninlil gave him a surprised look and asked, 'Why not?'

'I will leave only if you come with me,' Enlil said. 'I have fallen in love with you and want to marry you. Be my wife and you will have the most beautiful palace in the world,' he said.

But Ninlil thought he was too proud and arrogant. So she turned his marriage proposal down. Enlil, however, wasn't prepared to accept 'no' for an answer. So he turned into an eagle and kidnapped her. He took her to Nippur and there he married her.

When the older gods came to hear of Enlil's marriage, they were furious. Not only had he married without consulting them, he had also broken a sacred law by abducting Ninlil from her home and marrying her without her consent. So they banished Enlil to the nether world, which was hot and remained plunged in darkness all the time.

Enlil lived there in great misery. Meanwhile, Ninlil had fallen in love with her husband, so she decided to follow him to the nether world. There they lived, a little happy, a little sad and most of the time talking of when they would be free to return to their beautiful home.

Some months later, they had a baby. He was a beautiful

child who gurgled with laughter and radiated light and happiness everywhere he went. They named the child Nanna.

Enlil wanted his son to escape the suffering of the nether world. So he turned Nanna into a lamp and tossed him into the sky as far as he could. Nanna remained and became the light of the night sky. He slept all day and woke up only in the evening. Children and grown-ups alike waited for him to wake up, and when he did, they felt a great joy shoot through them.

Nanna loved his parents very much and every time he missed them, he went to visit them, taking with him to the nether world light and happiness. But the night sky would then loom over the earth like a big black menacing cloud, making little children cry and gods shiver in their homes. So they pleaded with him not to go away so often.

'Let my parents come back to their palace in Nippur and I'll never go away again,' he said.

The older gods were in a fix. They thought and thought and finally came to a decision. They called Nanna and said, 'We will let your parents come back to Nippur, but on one condition. Just so your father and the world don't forget that he broke a law, he will have to return to the nether world once in thirty days.'

Nanna was overjoyed and so were Enlil and Ninlil. But when the day came close for Enlil to go back to the nether world, he was frightened. Nanna decided to go with his father and from then on, once in thirty days, Nanna went missing from the night sky. But the rest of the days he glowed brightly—a comforting presence in the darkness of the night.

HOW MARSHLANDS CAME TO BE

A Siberian Myth

In the time before time was ever measured, the world had just been created by the great creator, Lord Ulgan. And in the beginning of all beginnings, once as he was walking through the clouds, he saw a strange sight. There was something floating in the primordial ocean. It had a face, but the rest of the body was shapeless. While the face remained intact, the rest of the creature's form changed as the waves rose and fell.

Now, Ulgan had always assumed that he was the only being who existed in the universe and was astonished to see another being sharing it. Unable to contain his curiosity and annoyance, Ulgan swooped down and asked, 'Who are you?'

The being changed shape a few times and then said, 'Who am I? That's a good question because you see, I don't have a name.'

Ulgan smiled. That was better. He would give the creature a name and that would make it beholden to him forever. 'I am Ulgan and no being ought to exist without a name. So, henceforth you shall be known as Erlik,' he pronounced grandly.

The creature gladly accepted this name and thereafter, a certain kind of friendship bloomed between the two of them. One day Ulgan asked Erlik, 'You have been to the bottom of the ocean. What is there?'

Erlik changed shape and became a mouth. Then he

said, 'Mud. Constant and stable and never changing. If you brought it to the top of the ocean, you could create countless creatures who could all live on it.'

Ulgan began to think. He was the creator lord, but he hadn't created much. It often made him worry. What kind of a creator was he if he couldn't have a few creations to his name?

'Erlik, are you my friend?' he asked.

'Yes.'

'Erlik, are you thankful that I gave you a name?'

'Yes,' said Erlik.

'Well, will you do as I ask?' Ulgan asked.

Erlik changed shapes to suggest yes.

'In which case, go to the bottom of the ocean and bring me the biggest chunk of earth you can find. I have an idea. I would like to create a world up here, above the ocean, and then I will create a few creatures to populate it.'

So Erlik changed shape and became a creature with a face and long hands and set forth for the bottom of the ocean to bring Ulgan a piece of the earth. When he had prised a huge piece to take to Ulgan, Erlik suddenly had a thought. Why don't I do the same? I will keep some of this earth for myself and create a world of my own, he decided. But his hands were full. So Erlik opened his mouth and bit off a piece of earth small enough to hide in his mouth.

Then Erlik floated to the surface and offered the piece of earth to Ulgan. Ulgan accepted it happily. He threw it onto the surface of the ocean and said, 'Now watch me!'

The piece of earth Ulgan threw on the water began to expand, growing bigger by the moment.

Erlik began to panic. What magic had Ulgan caused? The piece in his mouth was beginning to expand as well and soon he was starting to choke. Ulgan too noticed that

Erlik's face was changing colour. In a flash he understood what Erlik's plan had been.

'You are so stupid, Erlik,' he said. 'Did you really think you could get away with this? There can be only one creator and one world. Me and mine. Henceforth I shall not be your friend nor let you be among those I create. Since you so badly wanted to be king, you shall be king of the dead, of those creatures who have lost their souls. And now, spit out the piece in your mouth or you will die in the next few moments.'

Erlik felt anger and hate rise in him. But he had no option but to listen to Ulgan's words. So he spat out the piece of earth which joined the rest of the rapidly forming earth. However, since the piece of mud had remained in Erlik's mouth for a while, it became an unpleasant piece of land, wet and slimy, and became the boggy marshlands that appear all over the earth.

THE HUNGRY GHOST

A Legend from Borneo

Once Radin, the great leader of the people of Borneo, won a fierce battle at a place called Betong. Radin belonged to a tribe of head hunters. In the battle he took many heads and later, these were all displayed for the world to see and know the leader's bravery. To celebrate his victory, he decided to hold a bird festival during which figures of all the birds of Borneo and even mythical birds would be displayed. 'We will invite all the other warlords and the wise men of the region and we shall celebrate my victory over many days,' he told his men.

Soon preparations began and images of birds were made and placed all around the longhouse, which was home to the entire village. All the other warlords and the wise men arrived and the feasting began.

On the second day of the feasting, one of the wise men noticed that among the images of the birds, Radin had placed one of the rhinoceros hornbill—a bird sacred to the head hunters. He called Radin aside and said, 'It wasn't wise to make an image of the hornbill. But it isn't too late. When the celebration is over, you must remove the image and leave this longhouse forever.'

Radin agreed and when the festivities came to an end, he ordered the image of the hornbill be removed and left near the forest. However, it seemed too much trouble to build another longhouse, so Radin and his people continued to stay there. Some days later, a man fell ill. Giant pustules appeared all over his body and he lay writhing in pain and fever. By morning he was dead. A frightened murmur spread around the longhouse: small pox. The next day, seven people were stricken and the day after, fourteen. Radin was worried. What could be wrong, he pondered. Which god had he offended? That night, as he lay sleepless, he heard a song. The voice was beautiful and the singing melodious, but the words of the song made his blood run cold. For, the singer was celebrating death. Radin couldn't find who the singer was.

For three nights Radin heard the song and realized that this was no earthly visitor. On the fourth night, Radin hid himself. When the singing began, he crept out with his machete, which he had sharpened all day, and cut through the air. With one swinging motion he slashed the air and with another he swished the machete at the place where he thought the voice was coming from. Radin heard a scream and then the sound of something fall. But there was nothing to be seen when he lit a fire and checked.

The next morning everyone was well and all those who were ill seemed to have recovered. Radin was puzzled. Just then someone came running and said, 'You must come with us. You won't believe this.'

Radin went with the man and at the outskirts of the forest he saw that the carving of the hornbill lay damaged. There was a deep gash in the body and the head lay apart from its body. Suddenly Radin realized why the wise man had asked him to vacate the longhouse. The hornbill had attracted a ghost who had then chosen to make the hornbill's figure its home. At the feast, it had seen the people of the village and had made them food for its rapacious appetite.

Radin now realized his mistake in not listening to the

wise man's warning. Along with his men, he built a new longhouse. The old one began to be used as a burial ground thereafter.

THE STORY OF DHRUVA

An Indian Myth

Once there lived a king called Uttanapada who had two wives, Suruchi and Suniti. Suruchi was very beautiful and hence the king's favourite. This made her haughty and proud. Suniti was a quiet woman and not so beautiful, hence both the king and Suruchi treated her rather badly.

Soon the queens were pregnant and both gave birth to sons. Suruchi's son was named Uttama and Suniti named her son Dhruva.

Uttanapada was very fond of both his sons, but his love for Suruchi made him love her son a little more. He always favoured Uttama. If there was a quarrel between the two boys, he would take Uttama's side. But Suruchi was still not satisfied. She feared that the king might change his mind and give Dhruva the throne. So she found ways and means to make Dhruva's life as miserable as possible, hoping he would run away.

She put pebbles under his mattress so he wouldn't sleep well. She squeezed bitter gourd juice into his food and added salt to his drinking water. She rubbed the soles of his footwear with butter so that he would slip and fall. She even put a thorn under the saddle of his horse so that it would throw him when he went riding. But Dhruva continued to stay in the palace with his mother.

Every night, he would cry to his mother, 'Why is she

being so cruel to me? What have I done that she is so nasty to me?'

Suniti would caress his brow and say, 'Hush hush, my son. Don't let the tears fall. If she sees you cry, she will know that she has won. And you mustn't let her have that pleasure.'

Finally one day even Suniti ran out of patience. Enough was enough, she thought and decided to confront Suruchi. The next morning she went to see Suruchi and said, 'Why are you being so nasty to my son? What has he done to offend you?'

Suruchi tossed her hair and said, 'If you want to know, his being alive offends me!'

'Don't say such wicked things,' Suniti cried, horrified.

'As long as he is alive, he is a threat to my son. Do you think that I don't see him trying to become his father's favourite?' Surcuhi said angrily.

Dhruva, who was in the other room, heard Suruchi's words and decided to intervene. 'Please Mother,' he began.

'There he is, the flea! Trying to suck up to the king only to feed on his blood,' Suruchi said. Then she took a deep breath and added, 'Can't you see that the king doesn't really want you here? How can you be so shameless and stay on where you are not wanted?'

Suniti began to cry but Dhruva understood what Suruchi desired. He wiped his mother's tears and said, 'I do not want to be king. I do not want anything that is given to me. Whatever I achieve, it shall be because I worked for it. So you can keep the throne, the palace, the elephants, horses and everything else. Just leave my mother alone and do not torment her.'

Dhruva left the palace that night and went to a hermitage where he began to live as a hermit. He devoted himself to learning and began to perform various austerities.

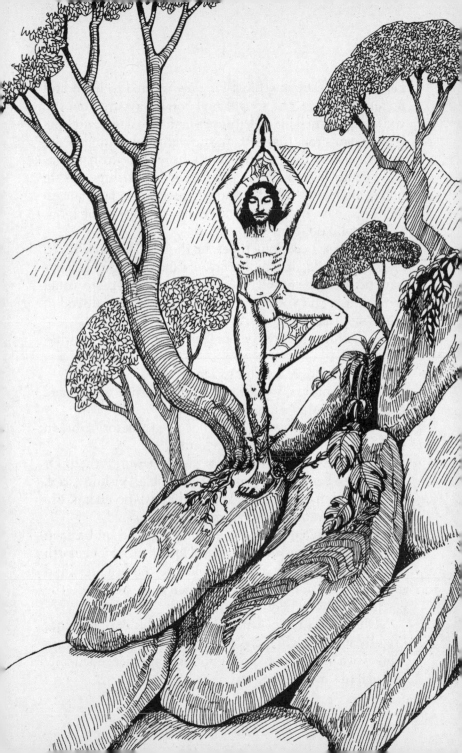

He did not desire anything. He only wanted to learn and understand life, so he sought no boon or favours from the gods. This worried Indra, because a man who desires nothing is more dangerous than a man who wants something. So he tried to disturb the penance, but Dhruva was unshakable.

Finally, Indra and the gods rushed to Vishnu, asking him to intervene. 'If he continues to perform such penances, he'll soon have heaven's throne even without asking for it. What shall I do then?'

Vishnu sighed. Sometimes, he thought, Indra behaved like a spoilt child, demanding favours and sulking if he didn't have his way. The problem was, if Indra sulked, there would be no rains, or he would go to the other extreme and send so much rain that there would be a flood.

So Vishnu appeared before Dhruva and asked him what he wanted.

'I do not desire anything,' Dhruva said.

'There must be something. Would you like to be made king of your father's kingdom?'

'I gave that up myself. What do I need that for?' Dhruva smiled. 'I really do not want anything.'

'Would you like to be king of the three worlds then? Or how about a boon that'll make you invincible?' Vishnu asked.

'No, I don't want to be king and I have no enemies so why would I want to be invincible,' Dhruva said.

Vishnu smiled. 'You are an amazing man and a man everyone ought to know about and look up to. Henceforth you shall be the pole star. You shall be the brightest and most constant star in the sky that shall guide people on the earth no matter where they are.'

Dhruva was happy with that and to this day, he shines brightly in the night sky. He can be seen every night, a symbol of a man who asked for nothing and succeeded only through his own hard work.

THE HARE ON THE MOON

A Buddhist Myth from India

When Brahmadatta was the king of Benaras, the Buddha was born as a hare in a deep forest.

The hare had many friends but his chosen group consisted of three animals: a monkey, a jackal and an otter. They were just as wise as he was, and often they sat together discussing many things.

One day the hare said, 'I have heard that there are certain days in a week when we must fast and give alms to the needy on those days. This fetches the alm-giver a place in heaven.'

The monkey nodded and said, 'Yes, I have heard this as well.'

Then the jackal said, 'In which case, why don't we practise it?'

The otter added, 'Yes, we must and I suggest we offer our food as alms.'

So on the first day of fasting even though they were very hungry, the four animals wouldn't touch a morsel and instead went in pursuit of food they could offer as alms. The monkey found some fruit; the jackal meat and the otter fish. But the hare went back to his burrow thinking, 'What use is this grass to anyone? How can I offer it as alms?'

So the hare decided that as he had nothing else to offer, he would offer his own body as food.

It is said that when a person's goodness exceeds the call of duty, the throne on which the king of heaven sits becomes unbearably hot. So hot, that the king is unable to even go near it. The moment the hare decided to give his body up as alms the throne started burning like a hot coal. The king of heaven looked below to see what had caused the throne to flicker and hiss. He heard the hare's resolve and decided to test if the hare really meant to keep his word.

Disguising himself as a poor brahmin, the king of heaven first went to the otter and asked for alms. The otter gave his fish readily. The monkey and the jackal too gave him alms when he approached them. Now it was the turn of the hare.

The hare smiled at the brahmin, pleased to see him even though he knew he would die soon. 'Brahmin,' the hare said, 'I shall give you alms like you have never had before. Would you gather wood and light it, please.'

The king of heaven made a fire and said, 'Here hare, I have done as you asked.'

'In which case, my time has come. When my flesh is cooked you must feast on me,' the hare said and flung himself into the fire. But the fire did not burn and died by itself instantly. The hare was puzzled. He turned to the brahmin and asked, 'What does this mean?'

The king of heaven smiled and said, 'I am no brahmin. I am the king of heaven. I came to earth to test you and see if you meant to keep your promise of offering yourself as alms.'

The hare bowed to the king and said, 'I fear that your efforts have been in vain. I shall offer myself to anyone who asks me for alms. I really mean to!'

The king replied, 'You must do as you see fit. But it is also your duty to live to the end of your destined life term. But I would like your generosity to be a lesson to the world.'

Saying this, he took the hare and gathered him under

his arm. In his other hand he picked up a mountain and then he rose above the moon. There, holding the hare against the moon, the king of heaven squeezed the mountain till its juice ran as ink, and with it he drew the outline of the hare on the moon where it stays to this day. All who see it know and understand that a little creature like the hare had such a great heart that the king of gods himself had to test him.

THE SNAKE'S SECRET

An Ethiopian Legend

After god in heaven created men and women, he discovered that as they grew old, they suffered a great deal of discomfort. Not only did their bones grow weak and their hair turn grey, they also lost the strength to feed and defend themselves. God was greatly distressed by this and decided to help mankind remain young, strong and healthy. So he called the bird Holowaka, who lived in heaven, and said, 'Holowaka, I want you to fly to earth with a message to mankind from me. Tell them, when they find themselves growing old, all they have to do is slip out of their skin and they will be young again. But remember to talk to no one on your way. If any other creature learns this secret, it will be theirs alone.'

So Holowaka promised not to speak to anyone or stop for anything on the way and set flight to earth. Holowaka flew for days and days and finally reached earth. By this time, Holowaka's wings were aching and his stomach felt all hollow and was rumbling with hunger. If I can get a tiny wee morsel to eat, then I can go on for some more time, he said to himself. But he couldn't find any food. When he was almost faint with hunger, he smelt meat. He went in search of it and found a snake feasting on a dead antelope.

'Please, could you give me some of the meat?' he begged. 'I've been flying all day and haven't had a bite to eat since last night. I just can't bear this hunger any more.'

The snake was a wily old creature. He knew Holowaka

was the bearer of some precious secret that god in heaven had entrusted him with. And he also knew that the secret would be only for man's ears. Now if the snake hated any creature, it was man. For as soon as man saw a snake, even a harmless one that was crawling along minding its own business, he took a stick and beat it to death. The snake had lost many a loved one in such a manner. So he sucked down a succulent piece of flesh and asked Holowaka, 'What will you give me in return?'

Holowaka looked around helplessly. What could he give the snake? Then he thought of his tail, which was long and coloured like the rainbow. He said, 'I can give you a feather from my tail.'

The snake snorted and said, 'What would I do with a feather from your tail? Wear it on my head? I want something else.'

'I can teach you to fly,' Holowaka offered.

'Pah,' the snake spat. 'No, thank you, I'm happy being on the ground.'

Poor Holowaka could no longer bear the hunger. So he thought hard and as he sat and wondered, he felt that with every passing moment he would die of hunger. Then he was overcome by a tearing rage at god. 'How could he send me on a mission without providing me enough food to eat on the way? All this is his fault,' he told himself and having comforted himself thus, he cleared his throat and said in a low voice, 'Snake, listen, I am entrusted with a great secret. This will change the life of mankind but now I am prepared to tell you the secret in exchange for food.'

The snake stared at the bird and then unable to hide his curiosity hissed, 'Go on, tell me . . .'

But Holowaka was clever enough to realize that the snake might trick him. 'You have to believe me . . . and I

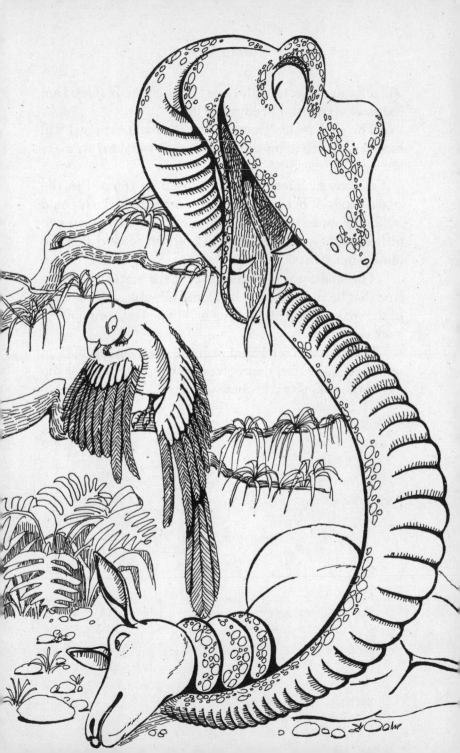

will tell you the secret only once I have eaten. Besides, I am too weak to speak. I need to eat first!'

The snake said, 'Come to me. You will eat but I will have to coil you in my clutches so that you don't fly away after you have eaten.'

Holowaka agreed and let himself be trapped in the snake's coils. When he had eaten as much as his belly could hold, Holowaka said, 'God sent me to say that when you feel yourself getting weak and old, all you need to do is slip out of your skin . . .'

The snake was so eager to see if the secret was really true that he slipped out of his skin. Holowaka felt the coils of the snake loosen and seizing his chance escaped quickly back to heaven.

But his secret remained with the snake and from then on, when snakes feel themselves growing old, they just slip out of their skins and become young once again.

HOW THE SKY WENT SO HIGH

A North American Legend

Mankind was very unhappy with the way the world was created. Not only did they all speak different languages that made conversation between tribes very difficult, but they also kept bumping their heads against the sky which was very low in places.

People often climbed up trees and went wandering into the sky world for days. When wives became angry with their husbands, they ran away into the sky world. When mothers told their little boys to mind the chickens, the boys disappeared for hours together into the clouds and came back saying, 'We ran after the geese who led us on a wild goose chase in the sky world.'

When clothes were hung out on clotheslines to dry, the wind took them away and hid them. One never knew where the clothes were, on the earth or somewhere in the skies scuttling behind clouds.

Finally, one day all the people went to the wisest man in the world and told him of the problems they were facing. 'It's because the sky is so low,' they said.

At first, the wise man thought they were making a fuss about nothing. 'I am sure you can all resolve it by yourselves,' he said. Just then, the wind who had followed the people to the wise man's house, decided to play a trick on him. He whipped the wise man's favourite black-and-red shawl from his back and left him shivering in the cold. 'Help, help, someone please fetch it for me,' he cried.

'Where do we look for it?' a boy asked.

'On the earth or in the sky world?' another girl asked.

'Go, go and look for it everywhere. By the time you come back, I will think of a plan,' the wise man promised.

So all the young men went looking for his shawl and found it many days later on the dark side of the moon. When they returned to the wise man's house, he took his shawl back from them happily and shook it to get rid of all the moon-dust on it. Then he wrapped it around himself tightly and said, 'Sit down, every one of you. Listen to me carefully. I know how we can solve this problem. When I give a signal, let us all push the sky up as far as we can, away from the earth.'

Since all the tribes spoke different languages, it was necessary to find a signal that everyone would understand. Once again, the wise man began to think. Finally he came up with a cry, 'YA-HOOSH!' Everyone liked the sound of it and began to prepare for the moment when the sky would be pushed up.

The day soon arrived. People from various tribes, birds and animals stood ready with long, hefty poles. The wise man cried, 'YA-HOOSH! YA-HOOSH!' And they began pushing the sky up until it reached the place where it is today.

However, a few people who did not know anything about the idea of pushing the sky had gone hunting that day. When they saw a herd of elk go up into the skies, they followed them into the sky world. As they followed the elk, the sky went so high up that the men and animals were stranded there. And that is how they became stars of the Big Dipper. On particularly clear nights, you can see them

trying to return to the earth, but they never succeed because the sky is so high and the earth so far below.

THE STORY OF TALIESIN

A Welsh Myth

In times long ago, there lived a very powerful witch in the black hills of Wales. Her name was Caridwen. She was very learned. She knew so much that if she ever wanted to write down all her knowledge, it would fill over a thousand books. After many years of study, Caridwen stumbled upon the recipe of a potion which would help her know all the secrets of the past, present and future. However, the potion would have to be boiled for a whole year before it was ready for consumption and then it would work only for the first person who tasted it. No more than three precious drops were needed for the person to attain the knowledge.

Caridwen didn't trust anybody to help her with the making of the magic potion. But even she knew that she couldn't tend the fire all by herself for a whole year. So she searched in the villages around her hut and finally chanced upon a boy called Gwion Bach who she thought could be trusted. He was an orphan and would be able to live with her in her hut.

She promised the boy many rewards and Gwion Bach agreed to be her helper for a whole year. He wasn't to see anybody or speak to anybody while he stayed with her. When his work was done, he would be free to go.

While Caridwen watched, day after day, night after night, Gwion Bach kept the fire going and gave the cauldron in which the magic potion bubbled, an occasional stir. The witch was pleased with her helper and began to leave him alone. Soon the year was almost up and the magic potion hissed and spat and bubbled. The witch knew the time was up and went out to prepare herself for the long awaited moment when she would learn the secrets of the past, present and future.

Just then the cauldron bubbled furiously and a few drops fell on Gwion Bach's finger. The boy, as was natural to do, sucked his finger and the three magic drops were consumed. In moments Gwion Bach realized that he was in grave danger and fled. The witch walked in a while later and saw that the fire had gone out. The cauldron was sitting as still as a pond.

'That little prat! How dare he!' she shrieked, turning purple with rage. 'There is only one thing to be done. I must gobble him up whole and all he knows will then be within me.' The witch said a magic chant that helped her locate Gwion Bach and she set out to capture him.

Gwion Bach sensed danger and turned himself into a beech tree. The witch went past him but suddenly she heard a man say to another, 'Have you seen anything like this? A fully grown beech tree has sprung up by the side of the woods.'

The witch turned into a woodman and brandishing a wicked-looking axe went down to chop the tree. 'I will light the wood and drink the ashes up,' she told herself. But Gwion Bach had already fled.

All around him were open fields and Gwion Bach didn't know what to do. Suddenly he sensed the witch nearby. So he turned himself into a grain but the witch was close at heels. She turned herself into a hen and pecked him with her beak. But just then a dog came and chased the hen. The grain fell out of the hen's mouth and dropped into a stream.

Gwion Bach now turned himself into a fish. The witch turned herself into a kingfisher. She swooped down and caught Gwion Bach. Then she rose into the sky and flew towards the sea. On a lonely spot somewhere she would swallow Gwion Bach whole, she decided. Just then a hungry gull saw the fish in the kingfisher's mouth and decided to snatch it away. So Gwion Bach as fish fell into the sea and was caught in a net.

When the fishermen hauled in the net, they discovered a handsome young boy. His brow was shining with the knowledge present in him and they decided to call him Taliesin.

He was taken to the king's castle. 'Who are you?' the king and his men asked.

Gwion Bach stepped back and sang, 'I am old, I am new. I have been dead. I have been alive. I am Taliesin.' Soon his knowledge and songs amazed everybody and he became famous in his land as the wizard bard of Wales.

CLOUDS IN THE SKY

A Papuan Myth

There was once a beautiful garden on the sea shore. Every day, a young woman came to the garden where there were trees and creepers festooned with flowers and hung with delicious fruits, where butterflies danced and birds sang and all day a soft breeze blew. The young woman plucked the flowers and feasted on the fruit. She sang songs and talked to the birds. When she felt hot, she swam in the sea and altogether spent a very pleasant time there. One day, seeing a beautiful big fish frolicking in the surf, the young woman too entered the sea and began playing with it until both of them were tired.

Several days later, the woman realized that the fish had rubbed against one of her legs while playing. That leg now began to swell. 'Father,' she cried, 'Please do something. I can't bear the pain any longer.'

Her father sharpened a knife and cut into the swelling. To their surprise, suddenly a baby popped out of it. His mother named the baby Dudugera. He grew up to be such a naughty boy that he became very unpopular. His mother feared that he would come to harm, so she decided to send him to his father, the fish.

On the way to the sea, Dudugera told his mother, 'Mother, I know that I have caused you much grief but I am unable to control my nature. Soon I will become the sun and trouble the world with the heat of my rays. I would like to make up for all the times I troubled you and your family

and so when I blaze down from the sky, you and your kin can escape if you take refuge under a great rock.'

As he spoke, his father the great fish appeared once more on the surf and carried him away. Dudugera's mother watched him go with sorrow. Then she rushed back to her village, where she gathered all her relatives and went to hide under the great rock.

As Dudugera had predicted, soon the sun's rays began beating down harsh and fierce. From under the shelter of the great rock his mother saw animals, plants and men droop and die in the heat.

She now realized that unless something was done, the whole world would be destroyed. So one morning as the sun rose, she went out into the open and threw sand into the face of the sun. The sand transformed into great white clouds and stayed in the sky. From then on, there have always been clouds protecting the earth from the sun's merciless rays.

HOW THE PING RIVER AND MOON RIVER CAME TO BE

A Thai Myth

There was a time when our world looked very different from the way it does today. Siam, or Thailand as it is known these days, was covered by an ocean that was deep as deep can be. In this ocean where even fish were scared to swim beyond a certain depth lived two mighty serpents. They were the rulers of the ocean. The northern part of the ocean was the domain of Pinta-yonak-wati and the southern part was ruled by Thana-moon.

Both Pinta-yonak-wati and Thana-moon were long of length and thick of girth and their appetites were as large as themselves. They needed a lot of food to keep up their strength and even more for their immense bellies to not feel hollow. The problem was that neither serpent could ever find enough food to satisfy his hunger.

Then one day Pinta-yonak-wati and Thana-moon met in the middle of the ocean. 'Hello brother,' Pinta-yonak-wati said.

Thana-moon arched his neck and nodded. He was feeling much too weak to even mouth a word.

'How are you?' Pinta-yonak-wati asked, surprised at Thana-moon's reticence.

Thana-moon mumbled, 'Very hungry.'

Pinta-yonak-wati sighed, 'I am hungry too. So hungry I could swallow a million sharks and still feel hungry!'

'Ah, that's exactly how I feel, except that I would need ten million sharks to take the edge off my appetite.'

'Have you ever thought how terrible this is? Here we are, two mighty serpents and rulers of this vast ocean and we are almost always hungry,' Pinta-yonak-wati said.

Thana-moon shrugged. 'I guess we'll die before it is our time, die of hunger!'

'Oh no, that can't be.'

'But what are we to do then?'

Pinta-yonak-wati smiled. 'I have an idea! Why don't we become a team? We'll both hunt for food. If I find something, I'll share it with you and you must do the same.'

Thana-moon smiled. 'That is a very good idea,' he agreed.

So for many days both Pinta-yonak-wati and Thana-moon ate well. One day, on Thana-moon's side of the ocean where there was an enormous mountain, an elephant lost its footing and fell into the ocean and was drowned. Thana-moon dragged the elephant to Pinta-yonak-wati and they shared it. For many days both serpents feasted on the dead elephant and didn't know what it was to feel hungry. But then came a day when Thana-moon said, 'Brother, we have no more food left. We must go and find some more.'

On Pinta-yonak-wati's side of the ocean were forests and fields. Only small animals lived there. But Pinta-yonak-wati waited for his chance and when a porcupine came to the edge of the field, he stretched his tail and grabbed the porcupine. He held the creature under the water till it was dead. Thrilled as he was by his prey, the serpent soon realized that the porcupine's sharp quills had injured his tail. Pinta-yonak-wati removed the quills one by one from his tail and then thought, 'These quills will hurt our mouths and insides. So I shall remove all the quills from the porcupine's body before I take them to Thana-moon.'

Carefully, Pinta-yonak-wati removed the quills and left

them in a little heap by the edge of the ocean. Then he called Thana-moon. When Thana-moon arrived, hungrier than ever, he was dismayed to see how small the porcupine was and thought, 'How will this feed the two of us?'

Then he saw the quills by the edge of the ocean and thought, 'Pinta-yonak-wati has been cheating me. He's already eaten as much of this beast as he wants. Now he is offering me a tiny morsel and pretending that he too must have his share from it so that I do not suspect him.' Thana-moon grew angry and said, 'You have cheated me. You have broken our agreement.'

Pinta-yonak-wati stared in surprise. 'Don't be silly. This is all there is of the porcupine.'

'I don't believe you. You are a cheat and a thief,' Thana-moon shouted. Losing his temper completely, he clouted Pinta-yonak-wati on the side of his head.

Now Pinta-yonak-wati grew angry and clouted him back. Soon there began a mighty battle.

Their fighting was so fierce that it caused huge waves to rise and many animals, birds and fish died. So loud was the noise they created that even the gods couldn't sleep. For seven days and seven nights the battle continued. When the animals, birds and fish and the gods could bear it no longer, they pleaded to Indra to help. 'Please, if you don't put an end to this, we will all die.'

Indra surveyed the serpents battling. Then he thundered, 'Listen to me, you foolish creatures. Stop this nonsense. Your battle has caused many innocents to die and much destruction. I order you to leave the ocean and go in opposite directions. Pinta-yonak-wati, you go to the north-west till you come to another sea, and Thana-moon, you must go south-east till you arrive at another. From now on those will be your homes. Go as fast you can, for in a day there will be no ocean here.' Then he turned to the fish and said, 'You must choose to go in whichever direction you want but hurry for the ocean will soon begin to dry up.'

Terrified at having incurred Indra's wrath, Pinta-yonak-wati and Thana-moon fled. Soon all the waters in the ocean dried up and the ocean bed rose till it became a piece of land, which came to be called Siam or Thailand.

As the serpents hurried to save their lives, their massive bodies left a mark on the wet earth. These filled with water from the rains and later came to be known as the Ping and Moon rivers.

WHY ALL LIVING CREATURES BEGAN TO WEEP

A German Legend

Odin, the oldest of the gods, was the god of battle, magic, inspiration and the dead. He had several sons and one among them was Balder. Balder was tall and handsome with rippling muscles. He was good tempered, kind and wise. Not surprisingly, Balder was his parents' favourite son.

One night as Balder lay sleeping, he dreamt of a green arrow that pierced the nape of his neck and lodged in his throat. The pain was excruciating and as the blood flowed, Balder knew that he was about to die. So real was the dream that Balder woke up screaming. Hearing him cry, his mother Frigg rushed in and asked, 'What happened? Why do you look so frightened?'

When Frigg heard of Balder's dream, she became very worried. In fact, she was so worried that she went to each and every living creature and extracted a promise that they would do nothing to harm her darling son. But there were so many plants and animals that Frigg forgot the mistletoe.

Now Loki, the mischief-making god and the father of lies hated Balder. All along, he had been planning to kill Balder. But with Frigg having made all living creatures promise to not hurt Balder, he found it next to impossible to make a weapon. Then he remembered the mistletoe and made a deadly spear out of it. With the spear in his hand, he went to his friend Hodr, a blind god, and asked him to hurl it into the mouth of the river where Balder was bathing.

Hodr was known for the power and accuracy of his throw in spite of being blind. Wanting to please Loki, he did as asked. The spear struck Balder on the nape of his neck and killed him instantly.

When Balder died, all the remaining gods became very unhappy. They felt lost without him and missed his laughter and wisdom. Then Frigg, his mother had an idea. 'If only someone went to the land of the dead where Balder is now, maybe we could buy back his life,' she said.

The land of the dead was really a prison filled with the souls of people who had died of old age, disease or accidents instead of in battle. Its queen was Hel and she lived in a magnificent ice palace named Sleetcold. Hel was a cruel woman and delighted in tormenting her prisoners. When Balder came to her prison, her joy knew no bounds. Here was her chance to get even with Frigg whom she considered her rival in beauty.

When Frigg came up with the idea of buying back Balder's life, his brother Hermodr went to Sleetcold. There he pleaded with Hel, 'Please let my brother Balder go.'

At first, Hel flatly refused, 'Once a soul comes here, I never let it go.'

But Hermodr wouldn't accept defeat and stayed at the gates of her palace pleading with her every time her chariot drove through the gates and past the place where he sat.

When many weeks had gone past, Hel began to tire of torturing Balder. So she decided to let him go. But in return, she wanted something that would make her feel happy always.

'Whatever you want will be yours,' Hermodr promised rashly, delighted at the prospect of getting his brother's life back.

'Well, in that case, I will let Balder return with you.

But from now on, I want to see all living creatures weep when they are in pain,' she said.

Hermodr agreed and that is how all living creatures began to weep. Since Balder was the reason why tears became a part of human existence, he came to be known as the Weeping God.

WHY THE WARAU INDIANS SELDOM BATHE

A Guiana Legend

Thousands of years ago, the creator decided that the best place to give to his creation, the Warau Indians, would be the heaven. So the Warau Indians made their homes among the clouds in heaven and studded it with stars as ornaments. There they lived very happily till one day a young hunter discovered a hole in the sky.

He crouched on his fours and peered through the hole. What he saw took his breath away. Beneath was a beautiful place with great green trees and flowing rivers, butterflies and flowers and luscious ripe fruits.

Excited by his discovery, the young hunter rushed back to his people, 'Hear hear my brothers,' he called aloud, 'I must tell you of this wondrous discovery I've made.'

So the rest of the tribe gathered around him and with amazement listened to his tale. Then they all went to the hole in the sky and peered down.

'We must explore this marvellous place!' they cried in unison and the entire tribe of men, women and children began descending.

Each one went their way to explore earth. Two girls wandered by themselves till they came to a forbidden lake. They stood by the waters of the lake and one of them said, 'It was all very nice when we peered at this place from heaven. But it is hot and dusty and I feel so filthy after our long walk. If I swim in these waters I shall feel clean again.'

'Don't,' the other one said. 'Remember what the elders

of the tribe said? We must be careful. They said we should not enter strange waters or caves unless they tell it is all right for us to do so.'

'Who will know?' the first girl demanded. 'As long as you don't mention this to anyone, I can have my bath and we can go back and pretend we were good.' Saying this, the first girl leapt into the waters with a cry of delight.

She did not know that the lake was the home of a water god. He woke from his slumber on hearing her splash about and gathered her in his arms.

The second girl waited and waited but the first girl didn't return. So she went back to where the others were and pretended she knew nothing about what had happened to her friend.

Some days later the first girl had a baby. As he had been born of a water god and a girl from heaven, he looked like neither. He was long and narrow with no legs or hands. He crawled and slithered and was at ease both on land and in water. So that his son could protect himself from harm, his father gave him a pair of fangs and a poison sac. The baby grew to become the father of all serpents.

Meanwhile, the Warau Indians had tired of earth. It didn't seem so wonderful anymore. It was hot and the ground at places was slushy. There were animals that growled and bit and insects that stung. Some plants made their skins itch and flies hovered around their heads buzzing all day. And suddenly there were serpents as well . . .

'Let's go back,' they cried and went to find the hole in the sky. But there wasn't a hole anymore. A fat woman who was always eating had got stuck in the hole and there was no way they could push her in or out.

As they stood wondering what to do, suddenly the skies boomed with the creator's voice, 'You, my people, were not content with heaven, and wanted the earth. But when you got the earth, what did you do there? You disobeyed me.'

The Warau Indians hung their heads in shame. The creator continued, 'You have spoilt the earth. One of you was responsible for filling the earth with serpents. Now you must stay there. There's no place in heaven for you.'

The second girl then narrated the story of what had happened to her friend long ago.

From that day the Warau Indians are extremely reluctant to bathe, for every time they see water they are reminded of how they spoilt the earth.

THE STORY OF THE SUN AND THE MOON

An Alaskan Myth

Long long ago, the sun and the moon lived as brother and sister in the Arctic zone. One winter, which was perhaps the coldest winter ever, the days and nights stretched endlessly. All the men were bored out of their wits. The women were busy mending clothes and stitching new ones, or combing their hair and fashioning ornaments from seals' teeth. But the men had nothing to do. They had mended their nets and sharpened their harpoons, repaired their sledges and even polished their axe handles. Now they just sat in their igloos twiddling their thumbs. It was too cold to hunt, too cold to go for a walk, too cold to do anything but brood on how bored they were and twiddle their thumbs all over again.

But more than anyone else it was the moon who was the most bored. 'I need to do something. I need to have some excitement,' he told himself again and again. Just then he spotted a group of women standing admiring each other's hair. That gave him an idea. 'Tonight when all the women are asleep, I will steal into their igloos and cut off a lock each from their hair,' he decided.

When it was time to go to sleep, Moon told his sister Sun that he wanted to take a little walk. 'Are you out of your mind?' she asked. 'You'll be frozen stiff!'

'I know,' he said. 'But if I don't get some air, I'll die . . .'

Sun sighed and went to sleep.

Moon waited till all the lamps were put out. Then he

stole into an igloo. One by one, the moon visited all the igloos and came away with locks of hair, which he stuffed in his pocket. But in the second last igloo he stumbled and fell, waking everyone.

The lamps came on and everyone saw it was Moon with locks of hair in his pocket. The women began to weep but the men were way too amused to be angry.

Sun was filled with horror, 'Shame has come upon our family. What shall I do?' she cried.

Now Sun was always rather excitable. She was aghast at what Moon had done and to show her penance for her brother's actions, she took a harpoon and mutilated her body before anyone could stop her.

'I have to pay for what you did to those other women,' she said and grabbing a torch she flew into the sky.

Moon was horrified by his sister's anger and wanted to comfort her. But she wouldn't listen. So he took another burning torch and chased after her.

As he ran after her in the sky, suddenly his torch went out, while Sun's continued to burn brilliantly. He never managed to catch up with her as Sun would never stop to speak to him. They lived in the sky in the same house but in different rooms, never seeing each other again face to face. Moon always thought of himself as the supreme deity but his torch didn't burn as bright, he could never be as brilliant as his sister.

THE NOBLE DOG

A Jataka Tale from India

Once there lived a homeless dog. It managed to live eating vegetables or even blades of grass unlike other dogs who feasted on human flesh in cemeteries. Since he was a pious and noble dog, the other stray dogs approached him and said, 'Sir, you're like a father to us. Please become our chief and protect us like your children.' The dog agreed to be chief and went about his duties righteously.

One day, the harness used for the royal chariots was left lying in the palace courtyards. That night it rained making the leather soft and chewy. The king's pack of hounds found it and tore it up. Finally they swallowed it.

The next morning, when the palace attendants found the harness missing, they were terrified. They told the king, 'It's the fault of all those stray dogs who enter our grounds. They have become a terrible nuisance, Your Majesty.'

The king was very angry that his harness was spoilt, so he ordered all the stray dogs to be killed. When they heard this, the dogs ran to their chief quaking in fright. 'Don't worry,' he said, 'the king has been told lies. We will tell him the truth.'

He led his pack through the streets and to the palace. The palace guards and attendants stood speechless as the dogs went past them and into the king's court.

Standing before the king, the chief dog spoke in a human voice, 'We have been wrongly accused, Your Majesty.

Give us a chance to prove our innocence.'

The king was awed by the behaviour of the dogs and by the presence of a dog that spoke like humans. 'You have my permission,' he said.

The chief dog continued, 'If Your Majesty will ask someone to feed the royal pack of dogs some grass and buttermilk, we will have the proof.'

The king was curious. 'What is the purpose?'

But the chief dog only smiled mysteriously and said nothing.

The royal packs were fed grass and buttermilk. Since dogs cannot digest either, soon they began vomiting pieces of leather.

The king was impressed by the chief dog's wisdom. 'I salute you,' he said, 'Let me have the honour of sharing a meal with you.'

The chief dog replied, 'Thank you noble king, but first grant me the promise that the lives of all living creatures in this kingdom will be spared henceforth.'

The king agreed and spread the lesson of ahimsa or non-violence wherever he went.

It is said that the chief dog was an incarnation of Buddha and the king an incarnation of Ananda, his chief disciple.

HORUS, THE DUTIFUL SON

An Egyptian Legend

In the ancient days, the gods of Egypt lived on earth along with man. Of the gods, Osiris was the lord of water and vegetation. He made rivers flow and trees bear fruit; he gave the jasmine its fragrance and the marigold its colours.

Osiris made the earth green and fertile, so naturally he was the most popular god. He was so well loved that his brother Seth became very jealous. One day, Seth could no longer contain his jealousy. So when Osiris was asleep, he captured his brother, shut him in a box and drowned him.

Everyone searched far and wide for Osiris but no one knew where he was. Three days later his body rose to the surface of the water and at last people throughout the world knew what had happened to him. Isis, his wife, wept and tore her hair out in grief. She knew Osiris had been murdered by Seth but there was nothing she could do.

As her grief became worse, her anger grew. 'I must have my revenge,' she told herself all day and night. Then using magic, she had a son who combined the best of her and Osiris's powers.

Afraid of Seth's wrath, she went into hiding in the marshes. There she raised her son, Horus, in utmost secrecy. The little boy grew up in the marshes with only frogs and birds for friends. His mother taught him all that he needed to know and gradually the years passed.

When Horus became a strong young man and could

wield weapons as well as any brave warrior, Isis told her son, 'Horus, you are the son of the Lord Osiris who was treacherously killed by your uncle Seth. It is because I fear him that I raised you in secret. Now the time has come, my son, for you to claim your right.'

Horus, who had always wondered what had happened to his father, now felt tears of sorrow and rage gather in his eyes. 'Mother bless me!' he cried, 'So that when I go into Egypt, I shall be able to avenge my father's death.'

Horus marched into Egypt, his handsome young face bright with a strange light. He stood outside his uncle's palace and roared to the gods to stand witness in the battle between him and his uncle.

Seth who had been asleep woke up with a start on hearing the thunderous roar. 'Who is that impudent boy?' he stormed. 'How dare he challenge me? I shall tear him into pieces.'

He rushed out of his palace to where Horus was waiting for him, prepared for battle.

Seth glowered at the young boy, hoping to scare him with his fierce stare. But Horus held his gaze and so the battle began.

First they hurled weapons at each other, then they resorted to tearing trees off the ground and fighting with them. Nothing was spared—rocks, clods of earth, the tails of the stingrays and wolves' claws—even thunderbolts and forks of lightning were used as they fought long and furiously. Then it suddenly seemed Seth was winning, for he reached out and plucked out one of Horus's eyes. Horus fell on the ground bleeding and in shock.

But then he picked himself up. 'I will not accept defeat,' the brave lad cried and plunged back into battle. After another long and bloody battle, at last Seth was defeated

and humbled.

Seth now restored Horus's eye. But Horus threw it aside and replaced it with the divine serpent which became the emblem of royalty.

After that terrible battle, Horus came to be known as the most dutiful son. As he represented the acme of power, duty, courage and honour, all the pharaohs of Egypt who came after him were thought to be descendants of Horus.

OSSIAN'S SORROW

An Irish Legend

In the Irish village where Ossian lived, they called him Ossian the hero. Each time he came back from his travels, the village folk stood outside their houses and lined the main road to admire this tall and strong man.

Ossian, they knew, was a hero who wandered far and wide in search of adventure. And that he came back alive and well to tell his tale made them respect him. Ossian would smile at the women and joke with the men and pinch the cheeks of the little children. Then he would tell them about his latest adventure. But after a few days, Ossian would crave for more adventure and he would leave.

One day, while walking in a deep and green wood filled with strange trees and plants and long shadows, he encountered a mysterious creature curled at the foot of a tree. Ossian stood there staring at the creature which was like nothing he had ever seen. It had the beautiful body of a woman and the head of a pig.

Ossian felt fear grip his heart. This is the devil in disguise, he thought. But unwilling to let this strange quarry escape, Ossian drew his sword. At that very moment, the creature opened its eyes and spoke to him in a voice softer than the feathers of a swan, 'Oh valiant hero, do not harm me. I am the queen of Fir Nan-Ogg, the land of youth. A spell has turned me into this obnoxious being. If you marry me, you will be able to break the spell. The pig's head will vanish that very moment.'

Ossian was so moved by her tale that he married her on the spot. As soon as he did so, the pig's head fell off and was replaced by the most beautiful face he had seen. Together they lived happily in the land of youth.

One day, Ossian felt faint stirrings of sorrow in him. He longed to see his home again. The sorrow grew in him every day. His eyes grew dull and he stopped smiling.

Unable to watch her husband's misery, the queen said, 'You have spent three centuries in this land of youth. Go if you must, my husband. But take care. You must ride a white horse and not touch the land at all until you come back. Or we will never see each other again.'

Ossian was filled with joy at his wife's words, 'Do not worry, my beloved. I will be back soon. I only want to see my home.'

He mounted a magnificent white stallion and galloped away. As he rode, he tried to forget the great sorrow he had seen in his wife's eyes. 'Why is she so unhappy?' he wondered.

Ossian's mind was so full of thoughts that he failed to guide the horse carefully on the slippery ground. Suddenly the horse stumbled and Ossian fell off. And in an instant the marvellous horse was dead and Ossian lay on the ground—a blind old man with only memories of the glorious home he had left behind in the land of the youth.

WISHPOOSH AND COYOTE

A North American Myth

Long long ago, there lived a monster who looked like a beaver and was called Wishpoosh. He lived in a large lake full of fish. Wishpoosh didn't let anyone fish in the lake and every time a fisherman came, he caught the man with his giant claws and yanked him to the bottom of the lake.

The people who lived in the region were sick and tired of Wishpoosh. So they pleaded to the trickster god Coyote for help.

Coyote had a very cunning mind. He thought for a long time and finally made a huge spear with a long strong handle and fastened it to his wrists with a flaxen rope. Then he went to the lake and pretended to fish.

Wishpoosh as usual tried to seize the god. But Coyote hit him back with the spear. He then chased Wishpoosh to the bottom of the lake where they fought fiercely. So fierce was their battle that even the surrounding mountains retreated. Wishpoosh tried to flee but Coyote speared the monster and together they began to flow downstream until they reached the Pacific Ocean.

Once there, Wishpoosh broke free and began seizing whales and eating them to renew his strength. Coyote lay on his back and floated trying to regain his strength. Suddenly he had an idea. Coyote changed himself into a branch of the fir tree and floated near Wishpoosh.

Wishpoosh in his greed ate the branch too. Once inside

his stomach, Coyote changed himself back to his normal shape and began hacking at Wishpoosh's heart until the monster was dead.

Now Coyote had another brilliant idea. Why let the enormous corpse go waste, he thought. So he used it to create a new race of people. These people later went on to constitute the many Indian tribes living along the north-western coast of America. But in his hurry, Coyote forgot to give the people eyes and mouths. Soon he realized his mistake and began putting it right. But by then his knife-edge had become so blunt that some mouths became crooked and some too large.

To this day, the Nez Perce Indians who live in Washington state, and who believe that they were one of the tribes to be born in this manner, say that is the reason why they have such ugly mouths.

THE EAGLE'S EGG

A Finnish Myth

At first there was only water everywhere. There was neither the earth nor the sun nor the moon nor the stars. Num the sky god hadn't yet decided how he was going to create a world. He sent as scouts birds through the skies so that they could tell him all that they saw.

The birds flew every which way and returned with news to Num. However, one eagle was ready to lay an egg and instead of flying back to Num, she searched for a dry spot where she could lay her egg.

Now Vainamoinen, the son of the air goddess, was a magician who could live in the ocean as well as the skies. Vainamoinen was fast asleep in the waters and only his knee stuck out. The eagle saw the knee protruding out and thought it was a good dry place to lay her egg.

So the eagle swooped down on the knee, made a nest and laid her egg.

Vainamoinen was fast asleep and did not have a clue that so many things were happening on his knee. All he felt was something moving on it. Irritatedly he slapped his knee, changed his position and went back to sleep.

The eagle watched in dismay as her nest broke and the egg fell into the water. The egg broke and knowing there was no way to save her baby, the eagle caused the yolk to become the sun and the moon and the pieces of the shell to become the earth and the stars.

HOW ISIS BECAME A CONSTELLATION

An Egyptian Legend

Re, the sun god, was the father of all men. When he created men and women to populate the world, he decided to give people differently coloured skins, different languages and lands. Since the Egyptians were his most beloved people, he gave them the river Nile, which would keep their land green and fertile. To appease his other creations, he gave them rain. 'When it rains, the earth will drink it in and all will be green and fertile just as it is in Egypt,' he told them and the people accepted his decision happily.

'You are the most powerful being,' they said, offering their thanks.

However, even the mighty Re had to fight evil, day in and out. Every night he was attacked by the most venomous and evil serpent of all. The battle that followed would last all night. But Re alone knew the secret to immortality and would always manage to escape from the coils of the dark serpent. When he emerged victorious, it would be morning once again.

Re knew that if the secret to immortality ever became known, he would no longer be able to win the battle with the evil serpent. So he kept it a closely guarded secret. Though many tried to find out what the magic chant was, they never succeeded. Often when Re came to know of some foolish mortal who tried to find his secret, he would chuckle loudly. For the secret chant was his name. Anyone who uttered the word 'Re' would become immortal. But nobody ever thought of it.

Isis was the daughter of the earth god Geb and the wife of Osiris, the god of water and vegetation. Though Isis was beautiful and wise, she was unhappy about being a mere mortal while the rest of the family enjoyed an exalted position. 'Why can't I be a goddess too?' Isis complained. But no one could help her become one.

'The only person who can make you immortal is Re. Maybe you should ask him,' her father Geb said.

Isis knew that Re would never tell her the secret to immortality but she was determined to be a goddess. So she thought and thought and finally hit upon a clever plan.

She collected some of Re's spittle, mixed it with earth and created a deadly serpent. She placed it on the path that Re walked on every evening. Then she hid behind a bush that was by the side of the path. Soon Re came walking that way.

Now Re was an old man whose eyes failed him in the evening. So he didn't see the serpent and stepped on it. As was to be expected, the serpent bit him.

Re fell down with a cry.

Isis had been waiting for this moment all along. She came out of hiding and rushed towards Re with a look of great concern on her face. 'Oh Mighty One,' she said. 'Save yourself before the whole world is taken over by the darkness of the evil serpent. Say that magic word before the venom seeps into your blood.'

Re had no option but to reveal his secret. 'Re,' he muttered in as low a voice as possible barely moving his lips. And soon he recovered.

As for Isis, she had been sitting so close to him, supporting his back against her shoulder that she too

received a portion of his power. And so Isis became immortal and later became the constellation of stars that we all know as Sirius.

WHY THE DAY ALWAYS RETURNS

A Myth from the Amazon Basin

A long time ago, the world existed in darkness. There was only night and the people were miserable all the time. Unable to bear their unhappiness, the people turned to the two brothers Kuat and Iae, the sun and the moon. But the brothers were just as helpless. 'We wish we knew how to create light. But the truth is, we don't know.'

The people protested, 'But you must find a way. Who are we to turn to if you don't help us?'

So the two brothers sat thinking, when Moon suddenly said, 'I have heard that in the village of the birds, they possess the day. If we were to steal it, then all our problems will be solved.'

'But how?' Sun asked.

The brothers thought for a long time and came up with an idea. They created an effigy and filled it with fat succulent maggots. Then they had a swarm of flies attach themselves to the effigy and take it to the village of the birds.

At first Urubutsin, the vulture king, couldn't understand where the humming sound came from. Then he spotted the effigy studded with flies. 'What is the meaning of this?' he asked his council.

One of his subjects, another vulture said, 'Let us break open the effigy and see what it contains . . .'

So the council pecked open the effigy and out popped the maggots. Urubutsin was delighted and fell upon them hungrily. When he had eaten every single maggot and the flies as well, the vulture yawned and sat back. One of the council members said, 'I think this is an invitation to our king and his family to visit the land of the people for a feast.'

'That may be so,' Urubutsin said. 'But I have eaten my fill and feel much too full to go anywhere. So why don't all of you go?'

'We could pass for your family,' the council member said. 'But what about the others?'

'Oh, shave all your heads and they'll think we are all from the same family with just some difference in size and colour.'

So the birds all shaved their heads and set forth to the land of people. Many hours passed.

Urubutsin grew hungry again when he heard a distinct humming. 'My subjects must have sent me a snack so that I don't grow hungry,' he thought.

Another swarm of flies came near and huddled on the ground. The vulture king spotted an effigy beneath them and flew to sit on it. The moment he sat on it, Sun and Moon who were hidden inside the effigy grabbed his feet and wouldn't let him go. 'You will have to be our slave forever and your subjects too unless you agree to our demand,' they said.

'What do you want?' Urubutsin asked, petrified at the thought of having to work.

'Give us day and we'll let you go free,' the brothers said.

The vulture king agreed. 'You may have day but if you always have day, then won't night be upset. Why don't you alternate the two? That way we will also get day . . . I promise you it will always come back.'

The brothers looked at each other. It made sense.

Having a never-ending day would be as much trouble as having night always. 'We accept,' they said, taking day back with them.

Since then day and night have always alternated and the vulture king has kept his promise too. He makes sure that the day always returns.

WHY MAN DID NOT BECOME IMMORTAL

IMMORTAL

A Mesopotamian Legend

The gods in heaven lay on their beds moaning and groaning. They had never known such suffering before—the sky, the moon, the stars and even the earth gods were hungry all the time and didn't know where to find food. So they lay in their beds and cried so loudly that it reached the ears of El, the father of gods who lived on Mount Saphon. El knew he had to find a solution.

So he called for a meeting of the council that consisted of Enki, the water god, An, the god of heaven, Enlil, the air god, and Ninhursag the earth mother. They gathered on Mount Saphon and began to think.

Enki, whose hands were never idle, was playing with a ball of clay. Suddenly he had an idea, 'Father,' he said with a shout of joy. 'I know what we can do. Let us create a being who looks just like us. He will be so grateful to us that when he asks us what we want, we shall demand that he worships us every day offering food. That way, all the lesser gods will never go hungry again!'

El was delighted by the idea and allowed Enki to fashion a creature who looked just like the gods. But he was mortal. He was called Adapa and so that Adapa might not be lonely, Enki created more mortals.

Enki's son Adapa became the king of the land and he ruled it wisely and well. One day, while fishing in the Persian Gulf, the south wind began to tease him. The boat tossed and turned and the waves rose as high as the boat's mast.

Adapa was furious with the teasing and he cursed the south wind. 'May your wings that cause me such trouble never rise again,' he said in a voice brimming with anger.

The curse was so powerful that the wings of the south wind broke. The south wind was so ashamed at what had happened that he never showed his face on the Persian Gulf. To this day, sailors know that when you sail on the Persian Gulf, there is no south wind.

After this incident, Adapa and his friends returned home safely. But the story does not end here . . .

The south wind that he had cursed was Tammuz, the son-in-law of An, the god of heaven. Tammuz complained to his father-in-law about Adapa's curse. So An summoned Adapa to heaven.

Enki heard about this and went to meet his son to prepare him for the meeting. He gave Adapa a tunic made of flax and said he should wear that instead of his tunic of gold. 'Be humble in your speech,' Enki said. Then he added, 'Son, don't eat or drink anything that An and his son-in-law offer you. For, even though they might pretend to forgive you, they will try and punish you.'

Adapa reached heaven and went to Tammuz's palace where Tammuz lay ill and in great pain. Adapa bent his head and fell on his knees, 'Oh Great God, we mourn your absence,' he pleaded, ' Forgive me for the sin I committed. Please pardon me and bless us with your presence again.'

Tammuz pardoned Adapa and An was so pleased by Adapa's frank admission of guilt and humility that he wanted to give Adapa a gift. He clapped his hands and a servant appeared. 'Bring the food and water of life,' he said.

But Adapa remembered his father's words and refused to eat or drink. 'I only want to go back to my land,' he said. So they sent him on the back of an eagle to Sumeria.

When his feet touched land, Adapa suddenly realized that he had been tricked by his own father. Enki had wanted to deny immortality to mankind so that they would always be inferior to the gods and never cease worshipping them with offerings of food. Adapa walked to his palace a sad man, knowing that in mankind's future lay death while he could have helped them live on forever by accepting An's gift.

WHY WE HAVE SPIT IN OUR INTESTINES

A Siberian Myth

The creator lord called Ulgan had Erlik, the water being, bring him mud from the bottom of the ocean. However, Erlik kept a piece hidden in his mouth and when Ulgan began expanding the mud, the piece inside Erlik's mouth also began to expand and he started to choke. Finally he had to spit out that piece of mud. Ulgan was very angry by this treachery and cursed Erlik to be the king of the soulless ones.

When the piece of earth had expanded enough, Ulgan waved his arm and the earth took the shape it is today. Now Ulgan decided it was time he created beings who would live on this newly formed earth. So he set about fashioning men and women, birds and beasts . . .

First Ulgan experimented with beasts. He made a dog with a smooth skin and gigantic jaws and breathed life into it. The dog shook itself and growled ferociously and this made Ulgan happy.

He then decided to create mankind. But he discovered that while he could fashion faces and limbs, teeth and eyes . . . get them to breathe and move, see and hear, they were no different from the dog. They needed souls. And he couldn't give them souls, as that was beyond his powers.

The awful thought also occurred to him that he had once told Erlik that all soulless creatures would belong to Erlik. What shall I do, he asked himself again and again. Is this what I went to all this trouble for?

Then Ulgan knew. He would ascend to the world above the skies, to heaven where the most supreme of all gods lived and he would ask him for help. Having made up his mind, just as he was about to set off, he realized that if he left mankind unprotected, Erlik might take them away. So he put the dog on guard and said to it, 'When I return, I shall reward you. But you must take good care and not move from here or let anyone take the humans away.'

Ulgan then left and as he had expected, Erlik arrived. When he tried to go near the incomplete mankind, the dog growled. 'Beware, I am on guard,' the growl said.

Erlik thought for a moment. Then he said, 'You are a very handsome animal. But when winter sets in, you are going to be very cold. Have you thought about that?'

Just then an icy wind blew and the dog shivered. Erlik sat down next to the dog and said, 'I could give you a beautiful golden coat but I need something in return.'

'What do you need?' the dog asked

'Nothing much. Would you let me go there and take a close look at what Ulgan has been creating?' Erlik said with an innocent face.

The dog thought a while. 'I can't do that. I would be failing in my duty.'

Erlik then said, 'I'll tell you what. You let me take one quick look and you can have your coat—a beautiful golden coat that'll keep you warm during cold days.'

The dog couldn't make up his mind. 'See here. You are not to cross this line. If that's fine, you can take a quick look. But first my coat, if you don't mind.'

So Erlik gave him a fine coat of fur and then waited while the dog drew a line. Erlik knew he couldn't take the people but he had another idea. He would taint and ruin them so that Ulgan would be forced to abandon them. So while the dog sat and admired his coat, Erlik took a hasty look at him and then gathering all his strength, he spat on the people and sped away.

When Ulgan returned, he saw his beautiful creation was quite spoilt with all the spittle that ran over them. He knew that Erlik had caused this. 'I am not going to give this up,' he thought, and he turned the bodies inside out. Then he blew into their mouths and whispered in their ears; he ran his hands over their skins and caused a light to enter their eyes. Thus he infused souls into the creatures. When he was done, he commanded them to awake and rise and they became beings who used their senses to distinguish between right and wrong. But there was something that Ulgan couldn't change. Since he turned his creations inside out to hide Erlik's spit, mankind has always had spittle in his intestines.

HOW JAPAN BECAME THE LAND OF THE RISING SUN

A Legend from Japan

Amaterasu, the sun goddess, was very angry with her brother Susanowo, the storm god. Susanowo was a very powerful god and his powers could make or break the world. So she had begged him repeatedly to be careful but he had paid no heed to her words. Instead, he neglected his duties and caused much havoc in the world.

He destroyed rice fields, uprooted trees and particularly enjoyed tearing down sacred buildings. Then, because he thought his sister was given too much importance, he made a hole in the roof of the hall where her maids sat to weave, and frightened all of them. Amaterasu's anger turned into a great fear then. She knew that her brother wouldn't rest till he had broken her powers and caused her great harm. She realized that he was beyond her control, so she hid herself in a cave and blocked the door with an enormous stone. It was then that the other gods realized the gravity of the situation.

With the sun goddess in hiding, darkness enveloped the world and evil spirits became more powerful. All the other gods were perturbed. The situation was getting out of hand.

In heaven, there existed a tranquil river which was supposed to calm the mind and help provide solutions. So all the gods held a conference on the bed of the river. There they decided that Amaterasu had to be brought out of the cave.

They found a great tree near the cave and decorated it

with jewels; cocks were released near the mouth of the cave
so they would crow all the time. A mirror, sword and cloth
were kept as offerings. Bonfires were lit and the goddess
Uzume danced to musical accompaniments. Uzume's dance
was so funny that all the gods present laughed till their bellies
ached and their laughter shook even the heavens.

The sun goddess in the cave heard the merry making.
'What can it be?' she asked herself. 'How can they be so
merry?'

She opened the door of her cave and called out, 'How
can you all be so happy in darkness?'

Uzume tossed her hair and replied, 'We are happy
because there is a more brilliant and prominent goddess
than the sun goddess.'

As Uzume spoke, two gods brought the mirror and
bowed to Amaterasu. Then they held it aloft and showed it
to her. The sun goddess was so bewitched by what she saw
that she let herself be drawn out of the cave. Only when
she stepped out did she realize that she had been looking at
her own reflection.

Meanwhile, another god stretched a rope of straw across
the entrance of the cave saying, 'You will never enter this
cave again.'

So Amaterasu reappeared and the world was bathed in
light and peace returned to earth. But she still hadn't lost
her fear of her brother's powers, so she stayed at the mouth
of the cave at night. The rope prevented her from going in
any further and first thing in the morning she would peep
out to see if her brother was far away. Then Amaterasu
would turn her gaze on her favourite group of islands, which
today is collectively known as Japan, blessing them with
her life-giving rays.

And so Japan became the land of the rising sun.

HOW DEATH CAME TO STAY

A Myth from Rwanda

For the Banyarwanda people who live in Rwanda in Africa, the universe is divided into three parts. There's a part above the sky, a part beneath the soil and a part in between. The whole universe, they believe, is growing old and is in danger of collapse were it not for the power of Imana. Imana knows all things and is the protector of everything. He is very powerful and has long arms.

Once, there lived a man who borrowed beans from everyone and when it was time to repay his loan, he made excuses and prolonged the debt period. One of the people that the man had borrowed from was Death. One day, Death was very hungry and decided to seize the man and eat him for breakfast. The man shook with fright and called Imana to come to his rescue. So Imana with his powerful arms grabbed the man from Death's jaws and saved him.

By then, Imana was tired of Death's cruelty and decided to hunt him down forever. So he called all men and women and said, 'Tomorrow I am going to hunt Death. I would like you all to remain inside your homes so that he alone is out and shall find no hiding place.'

The people agreed and went home. The next day dawned and the hunt began. A little later an old woman sitting in her home felt a great yearning to suck the nectar from a banana flower. She looked out. No one was around. If I slip out and slip back in, no one will know, she thought and opened the door of her hut and stepped out. She walked quickly to her banana grove and just then Death appeared there. He affected a piteous voice and said, 'Please mother, please hide me. I don't want to be killed. I really mean no harm to anyone and I don't understand why Imana hates me so.'

The old woman, like many the other people, had never encountered Death and did not know what he could really do. She thought Death was quite harmless. 'Oh, the poor thing, I will hide him!' she said.

Just then they heard Imana fast approaching. 'Here, come,' she told Death, 'I'll swathe my skirt around you and Imana will not know where you are.'

So she hid Death and when Imana came looking, Death was nowhere to be seen. But in a few moments, Imana knew what had happened and he was very angry. He summoned all the people and said, 'If I had killed Death today, you would have been immortal. But one of you chose to harbour Death and to hide and protect him. Since you like Death so much, he will stay amongst you for as long as there is this universe.'

And that is how Death came to stay in the middle world.

WHY THE BEAR'S TAIL IS JUST A STUMP

A Swedish Legend

A long time ago, there lived a man who went around the countryside selling fish. One day, as he was driving his cart through a deep, dark wood, a fox set out in search of food. 'Aha, ha,' the fox thought. 'I smell food. I smell herring!'

The fox jumped onto the back of the cart as silently as he could and began eating the fish one by one. The man continued driving his wagon not suspecting that the fish in his cart were disappearing into the fox's belly.

The fox would have eaten all the fish except that he crunched a fish head rather too loudly. The man turned in surprise. There he saw, sitting in his cart, a fox with a fish in its mouth. He lost his temper and hit the fox with his stick.

His blow was so strong that the animal fell off the cart and lay on the ground. The man now stopped his cart and went close to the fox who lay in a little heap unmoving and, it seemed, not breathing.

The man prodded the fox with his boot and thought, 'Since the fox is dead, I might as well take him and sell his skin. It will fetch me enough to make up for all the fish he's eaten.'

So he put the fox back in his cart and began driving. A little later the fox opened his eyes. He felt the bump on the side of his head and decided to get even. Very quietly he began throwing the fish from the cart.

When there were just a few fish left, the fox jumped

out of the cart and began gathering them. Soon he had a huge mound of plump fish and he ate them one by one savouring each mouthful.

As he enjoyed his meal, a bear came by. The bear wasn't particularly hungry. But he was very greedy. He stared at the fish in surprise and said, 'Where did you get all that fish from?'

The fox thought quickly. He had to get rid of the bear or else the bear would gulp down all the fish in one big mouthful. 'Oh these,' the fox spoke airily. 'I got them when I went fishing yesterday.'

'Fishing?' the bear asked, amazed at the fox's luck.

'I know a very nice spot where the fish are fat and greedy and quite stupid. You can fish as many as you want. Why don't you? These are yesterday's fish and won't taste as good as the ones you catch today.'

The bear thought for a moment and said, 'But what do I fish with?'

'Very simple,' the fox replied. 'Fish with your tail just as I did. You make a little hole in the ice. Then let your tail down into the hole and sit there till you feel the fish biting. But you mustn't take your tail out when you feel the first bite. You must wait. Soon many fish will do as the first one. At that point you must whip your tail out, shake it and there will be a fine catch, all just for you.'

The bear's eyes gleamed at the thought. He decided to do as the fox said and made a hole in the ice. There he sat with his tail in the hole dreaming of countless fish, plump and tasty.

Then he felt the first bite. Yes, yes, he thought, the fish are biting. What a splendid meal I will have! Remembering the fox's advice he continued to sit there till he thought there were several fish dangling from his tail. Then in one

swift motion he whipped his tail out. But when he turned, he saw that the ice had trapped his tail leaving him not only with no fish but also just a little stub of a tail. Since then bears have always had small stubby tails.

THE BALANCE BETWEEN
LIFE AND DEATH

A Myth from Japan

At first there was only an ocean of chaos and in that sea of churning foam lived Izanami the female goddess and her brother Izanagi. The brother and sister together created the earth and heaven and then gave them the sun, moon and storms. Now there was one more primal force that needed to be created: fire.

'Brother, it lives within me,' said Izanami. 'I shall give birth to it and then we need to work harder than ever so that our creation will be complete. We will need to create living creatures . . .' she said.

However, while giving birth to fire, Izanami died and was taken away to a deep dark place beneath the ocean, where neither the sun nor the moon nor even her child fire was allowed entry. The darkness was total.

Izanagi grieved for her and as his grief grew he decided that he couldn't allow his sister to die and leave him. So he made up his mind to travel to that deep dark place and bring her back.

When Izanagi reached Yomotsu-kuni or the Land of Gloom as it was called, he was greeted at the gates by a voice. It was Izanami's. 'Brother, what brings you here?'

'Our work of creation is incomplete and without you it will remain thus. So it is my duty to come in search of you and take you back,' he told her.

'I understand,' Izanami said. 'But I must ask permission from the gods of this Land of Gloom and if they let me go,

I shall come with you. There is one condition, though,'
Izanami added.

'And what's that . . .' Izanagi said, willing to say yes to
anything as long as his beloved sister Izanami went with
him.

'Do not enter this land. You must stay where you are.
You mustn't ever look at me again. I shall always follow you
and only when I say so, you may look at me.' Izanami said.

Izanagi agreed and sat on his haunches waiting for his
sister. Much time went past but Izanami did not emerge.
Soon Izanagi became restless.

He took a comb from his hair and broke one of its teeth.
Then he lit it and using it as a torch, he entered the Land of
Gloom.

Izanagi was not prepared for what met his eyes.
Everywhere there was decay. Maggots and worms crawled
all over the place and the stench filled his nostrils. To his
horror he saw that Izanami too wasn't spared. She was
rotting.

Izanagi flung his torch down and ran away as fast as he
could. As Izanagi ran, he realized that a horrid-looking old
woman with wings for feet was chasing him. He didn't know
who she was but he realized if he fell into her hands that
would be the end of him.

He ran and ran and the hag chased him till he was
almost out of breath. Then Izanagi pulled off his headdress
and flung it to the ground. The headdress became a bunch
of grapes which the hag stopped to eat. Next when he
thought she was almost catching up with him, he broke his
comb and scattered it on the ground. These became bamboo
shoots which the greedy old woman stopped to devour.

Now there was only a little distance left between the
land of the living and the land of the dead. So Izanami,

who was very angry with her brother for having seen her rotting form, sent eight thunder gods and an army of fierce ghoul warriors to stop him. Izanagi managed to reach the pass separating the two lands. There he defeated the army by flinging three huge peaches at them. Then he shut the pass with a huge rock and paused to catch his breath.

Soon he heard Izanami at the other side. 'Open this, Izanagi,' she said.

'Never. You are to stay where you are.' Izanagi said with a shudder. 'There is no place for you here. You belong to the land of the dead.'

'If you don't open this, I shall put a curse so that a thousand people die in your land every day.'

'In which case, I shall cause one thousand women to give birth to babies every day,' Izanagi said.

And so it happened. The brother and sister never met again but their wish came true. To this day when someone dies, somewhere else a baby is born and the balance between life and death is always maintained.

TALKING BROUGHT ME HERE

A Nigerian Legend

Once, a hunter went into the bush looking for prey. He walked for a long time but didn't find any animals. Suddenly he saw a skull. It lay beneath a tree all by itself. The hunter was so surprised that he began talking aloud. 'What could have brought just a skull here?' he said.

To his utter amazement the skull spoke up and replied, 'Talking brought me here.'

The hunter was so excited by the talking skull that he ran back to the village. He rushed to meet the king and said, 'Your Majesty, when I went in to the bush today, I saw a unique thing, a talking skull, my lord.'

The king was baffled. Is the man mad, he wondered. But the hunter persisted. So the king said, 'I'll send my guards with you to the bush to see if you're speaking the truth.' The king then secretly ordered his guards to kill the hunter if he had lied.

The hunter and guards went into the bush. They reached the tree beneath which the skull lay. The hunter now asked the skull, 'What brought you here?' But the skull didn't reply. The guards looked at each other knowingly.

The hunter pleaded, 'Please talk, skull. Or the king will have me killed.' There was no reply. All day the hunter tried to make the skull talk, but not a word did it speak.

When evening came, the guards refused to let the hunter go, 'You have spoken a lie. So here you'll stay and

keep the skull company.' They killed him and walked away.

Now the skull asked, 'What brought you here?'

The dead hunter's head replied, 'Talking brought me here.'

HOW FOOD CAME TO BE COOKED

A Myth from the Admiralty Islands in the Pacific Ocean

Once upon a time, a woman went looking for firewood in a forest. She was very beautiful and had a sweet voice as well. She sang as she went about her work. In the very same forest lived a powerful and wise snake. The snake was asleep when he heard the woman's footsteps and then the beautiful singing. He peered to see who it was and fell in love with her.

The snake slithered out of his house and said, 'You are very beautiful.' The woman blushed.

'Will you marry me?' the snake asked. 'I shall make you the happiest woman on earth.'

'But how can I marry a snake?' she asked.

'Don't worry. Every day for four hours I shall be a man and then we will be husband and wife. At other times, I will be a snake.'

The woman thought for a while. She disliked all the men in her village anyway and wouldn't marry any of them. Besides she was quite bored with life itself. This seemed a way to bring excitement into her dull life. So she agreed and the woman and snake were married.

Soon she had two children. A boy and girl. The snake loved his children more than anything else and was scared that the woman would corrupt them with the ways of humans. So he called the woman and said, 'From tomorrow I shall cease to transform into a man. I suggest you return to your village, or you will be bored and lonely here.'

'But what about the children?' the woman asked.

'They will stay with me. You can start a new life easily if you don't have the children with you. Besides, I have some things to teach them. When it is time, they will come to you.'

So the woman went away. The snake looked after the children till they were big enough to do their chores. One day, he called them and said, 'I would like you to go and catch some fish. Then I want you to cook it yourself and we shall all eat it.'

The boy and the girl went out. They caught fish quite easily but were not interested in cooking the fish. So they held it up to the sun and let the sun's rays heat it. Then they ate the fish with its scales, raw and bloody inside.

The snake saw this and was saddened. And afraid too. Once they develop a taste for raw flesh, what is to prevent them from grabbing me and eating me up, he thought.

So he called the boy and said, 'I am going to open my mouth very wide. I want you to crawl inside me.' The boy stared at his father, suddenly scared.

'Www . . . why?' he stammered.

The snake smiled. 'In my belly you will find fire. I want you to crawl inside and bring it out and give it to your sister. Then you must collect yams and coconut and bananas. After you have done that I shall tell you what needs to be done.'

So the boy did as asked and the two children gathered the vegetables.

'Now,' said the snake. 'I suggest you cook the vegetables by holding them above the flame.'

They did that as well.

'Taste it. Tell me which is better? What you ate once, or this?'

The boy and girl ate the cooked vegetables and found

it the most delicious food. 'This, this, this . . .' they said eagerly.

'Well, in that case, you must cook all your food henceforth,' the snake said and the boy and girl agreed. Later when they went to live with their mother, they spread the practice and that is how we all began to cook our food.

HOW MOUNT FUJI BECAME A VOLCANO

VOLCANO

A Japanese Legend

Long ago, an old man who grew bamboo trees on the slopes of Mount Fuji was walking admiring his trees, when he heard a cry. The old man knew that there were no humans living on the mountain and thought it was a kitten mewing. He kept walking but he heard the cry again.

Unable to bear his curiosity he walked in the direction of the crying. And there in a flat basket swathed in a beautiful silk cloth, he found an infant. The infant was very beautiful and the old man took her in his arms. Henceforth I shall tell everyone that she's my daughter, he thought to himself and took her home. He named her Kaguya-hime.

The old man raised the child well and taught her all the arts and skills. When she grew up, she was not only the most beautiful girl on earth but a very accomplished one.

Soon I shall have to find her a husband who is her match in looks and talent and good nature, the old man thought one day. Just then he heard a noise outside. When he peered through the window, he discovered that it was the emperor with his entourage.

The emperor had come to Mount Fuji to admire the bamboo trees and listen to the rustle of their leaves. As he walked through the bamboo groves, the emperor spotted Kaguya-hime and fell in love with her.

The emperor sent his ministers to the old man asking for his daughter's hand in marriage. The old man scratched

his beard and said, 'The emperor's a good match I know. But I will agree to his marrying Kaguya-hime on one condition. I have always fulfilled her every wish. I would like him to promise me that he will do the same.'

The emperor agreed and the marriage was celebrated with great pomp and ceremony. For a while, the emperor and Kaguya-hime lived in great happiness.

One day, seven years after their marriage, the princess told her husband, 'Beloved, I have to reveal a secret. The time has come for me to tell you that I am not a human. My home is in the heavens. And as per the decree of heaven, I shall have to return to my home.'

The emperor cried, 'How can I live without you, the breath of my life?'

The princess wiped his tears and gave him a mirror. 'It is a magic mirror. Look into it whenever you miss me and you will see my face.' And then she went away.

But the emperor couldn't bear his unhappiness. Carrying the mirror, he began to follow her to heaven. He climbed Mount Fuji till he reached the top but he couldn't find his beloved wife there, nor could he climb any higher.

His agony at losing Kaguya-hime was so great that his sorrow burst out of his body in great flames and set the mirror on fire. From that day onwards, smoke has always risen from the top of Mount Fuji and all who see it know that the smoke comes from the embers of the flame that once burst out of the emperor's heart.

HOW WHALES, SEALS AND FISH WERE BORN

An Eskimo Myth

In a world where there was ice and more ice, there lived a family of giants. They had many children. The youngest one was a girl called Sedna. All was well in the beginning when Sedna was a baby. But in a few years, even her parents were unable to manage her. The neighbours complained about her wild behaviour and everyone kept a safe distance. No one knew what Sedna would do next.

She shook a ladder when someone stood on it cleaning the skies. She chased the chickens till they were forced to turn into clouds. She twisted fully grown tree trunks till the bark became ungainly and misshapen. She pulled out young trees by their roots just for the fun of it and used the roots to tickle her father's nostrils when he was asleep. She spared nothing and no one. But the worst was her appetite for flesh. She ate everything her mother cooked and all that her father brought home from hunting. She stole from the neighbours' kitchens and some days was seen spying on their livestock and even their babies hungrily.

The neighbours held a meeting and went to see Sedna's parents. 'It grieves us to tell you this. But you must keep Sedna at home and not let her roam free,' they said.

'She is just a girl. A little wild . . .' her parents replied, trying to justify her behaviour.

'Please,' the neighbours said. 'We are not fools. Sedna is dangerous and we don't know or want to know what she will do next. She may be your daughter but she is a malevolent creature and we won't let you impose her on us.'

So Sedna was not allowed to go out. She hated being confined at home. She sat brooding and growing hungry by the moment. One night, when her parents were asleep, she looked at their plump calves and felt a great pang of hunger. She went close to them and began to gnaw on her father's leg. The giant felt sharp teeth clamp on his flesh and then a searing pain. 'What?' he screamed and woke up. Sedna's mother too woke up and they discovered that Sedna was actually chewing on the piece of flesh that she had torn off from her father's calf. They looked at each other in horror.

'The neighbours were right. She is dangerous. We must send her away,' her father said.

'But where?'

'First we must tie her up and then we'll talk.' They grabbed Sedna and bound her tightly.

Sedna's parents took her in a boat far away into the ocean. 'Untie her and we'll throw her into the sea. Let her go down to Adlivun, the land of the unholy dead, at the bottom of the sea and she will never trouble us or anyone again,' her father said to her mother.

They untied Sedna and threw her into the seas. But Sedna clung to the side of the boat and wouldn't let go.

Sedna's father shouted, 'Let go.'

Sedna screamed back, 'No, I won't and when I haul myself into the boat, I'll eat both you and mother up!'

Hearing this, Sedna's father drew out his axe and severed her fingers one by one so that she could no longer hold on to the boat. Slowly Sedna sank to the bottom of the ocean where she lives till today keeping guard over the dead.

As for her fingers, when they fell into the sea they became whales, seals and shoals of fish. Since then the Arctic Ocean has always been home to lots of whales, seals and fish.